LIVES OF THE SAINTS
(STORIES FROM THE BIBLE)

Michael Marcinkowski grew up in Detroit and lives in Bristol.

ISBN: 978-1-916938-62-5

Cover designed by Aaron Kent

Edited and Typeset by Aaron Kent

Broken Sleep Books Ltd
PO BOX 102
Llandysul
SA44 9BG

CONTENTS

Lives of the Saints

Michael Marcinkowski

Broken Sleep Books

'We who are not yet the living.'
'What comes after sainthood?'

POSTSCRIPT TO *LIVES OF THE SAINTS*

'As such the crush the Lord our God whose
chaunce like grief veil plait drownt death.

Haecceity "just this" the chaine of chalice
Rome vom fear buck leave gland sear and

truss in martyr's weave. Agone hap burnt
as Passion's Lot, hwaet penss lack waft in

wither wake blear solum mark not knowing
known as diaphragm the cannon's march

to poem begg and vanguard soil rotten
breathe as groaning crush and blaring doubt

> *selah*
> *selah*
> *selah.'*

LIVES OF THE SAINTS

I
NUMBER ONE

Which might just be something specific to the afterimage
of an empirical society and I guess it's a question of
whether or not there's much value in worrying about
methodology or thinking about the question of social
organisation and no matter what we might want to say
about management or teleology they're both just
dependent on the question of cause and I had stupidly
thought that Arnold's book was going to be about the
variability of culture and how it exists previous to our
understanding of it or the way that culture is nothing
except a refactoring of the non-sensible into the sensible
but really he just seems to talk about reticence and
cause and I guess it's that 'I think that the artists who
aren't very good should become like everybody else
so that people would like things that aren't very good'
which is still just that the intelligibility of anything is
always just the intelligibility of some previous state of
affairs which is still really just only about an older belief
in a particular understanding of the movement of time
which to me is only just a bare and somewhat foolhardy
commitment to the lasting efficacy of cause.

II
OR THAT

it's the readability of the poetic line or more than any-
thing it's the lyrical proposition of the thing and no matter
my feelings toward you or the collective will of ours toward
history or the balkanisation of the state it's forgetting

which is the supposed progressive idea of language
being the bulwark of memory and trace or the recognition
of trace and the repetition in which it's the very idea of
trace that is underwritten in the perspectivist longevity
of trace and it's that repetition is itself just change in the
longue durée which as in the contextualisation of the thing
or the actual density of a line built up and the particular
coherence of gravity none of this being choice but only
our situation being previous to the invention of the ideal
or the repetition of form which in the opposition to a
monist realism there's nothing that we can say about
the line other than that it's just the return of the same
which laid out across the moment of the lyric is change.

III

all of which is just the question of whether or not we
can have some criteria against which the poem is able
to be judged or the idea that there is an outside to the
informational question of judgement or the communica-
bility of judgement and it's about the supposition of
certain sets of particular facts which is really just a
question of judicial selection or the bracketing off of
certain parameters toward the claim of phenomenolog-
ical experience and in that there's a need for the delineation
of certain understandings of horizon or the possibilities
of the repeatability of phenomena which are not such
as the specificity of texture or the absence of texture but
for some reason I always think that you're unhappy with
me or that I'm somehow screwing things up and it's that
I don't seem to have any real purpose with things and
maybe there are other methods of reparative behaviour
or things I could do differently but the difficulty is maybe
to be able to feel the quality of a work without any recourse

to empiricism or the supposed coherence of reason or as
to be able to measure the absence of an historical trace that
being the central problematic in the differentiation of cause.

IV

Which is explainable to what largely and it's intimidating
to think about the wholeness of a poem or the image of
a poem or at least academically and I wonder if you had
ever imagined New York differently all those years or at
least in the articulation of things as we think about them
to ourselves and it's the description of the poem to itself
or as accidentally to thyself of the egalitarian of the existing
and non-difference and 'one night I dreamed that I painted
a large American flag and the next morning I got up and I
went out and bought the materials to begin it and I did'
which as with realism is the impulse of difference and
maybe this is the logic of the poem which is difference or
the similarity of the image of the state to its memory instead.

V

and despite their own problems Western democracies
seem to be less capable of managing themselves
these days and maybe saying 'these days' is a bit
short-sited or is ignoring too much and it's like Clause-
witz or Foucault's reading of C. or like how information
systems are never a solution to material problems
or like the way that politics has been subsumed into a
more general physicality of intents and causes and I
mean is politics even a thing anymore like it was in
2006 or in the hangover of the post-Soviet years and
maybe it's not even a problem of democracy but it's
about the incapability of politics and the question of

how to manage anything other than just by the sheer
force of it and I guess I hope that there's some way
we can organise ourselves better in the future or I mean
is it even an epistemic question anymore or is it just
that there's no possibility for the management of change
and maybe we just shouldn't worry about things or
maybe it's really just that Hayek's theories about markets
and pricing signals were always just fucked up anyway.

VI
WAS DECIDED

II.

As to gauge against the true democratic question
of how many times an election may be run
until an answer's decided as the grandeur of
democracy is that it is able to be changed from one
moment to the next as the belief that any particular
event may not preclude any future occurrence as
democracy is weighted by its expedience to change
both as a benefit to and its mandate that if nothing
can be done in the span before the next vote then
it is not a thing to be done as there is no lasting
decision possible in a democracy or whatever
except the [uhh] continuing stranglehold of the state.

VII
for Harold Garfinkel

Dependence on the already established.

VIII
WHY ISN'T EVERYTHING ALREADY PERFECT?

Why does anything need to be changed?

IX

The anti-literary implication of the the thing or to say
that writing isn't any different from occurrence or the
way that the figure of the earth pushes down against
itself or the drag of the tide and it's the opposition to
cause that makes reading so resistant to an interiority
of logic and really there's no such thing as the specificity
of space or it's like how distance is only observed in
inscription or as part of a higher order proof which is
nothing other than the effect of occurrence itself and it's
unable to be recognised in the same way as abstraction
or the colonising of judgement which is always just
between the sun and myself or maybe just the remainder
of some radical doubt hanging over from the difference
between absorption and reflection and the moving of
visible light from one body to another and it's only that
context is the time that chance takes which is to say
that distance and effect are a matter of principle and

X
SOMETHING SOMETHING DECENCY RESPECT

Discomfort at the dawning of no borders newness
that some people are not ready for no borders
nor governance equality liberty such as the
joke of democracy's decency leniency threaded
back to tourniquets or the assembly of a *Jacobin*
Spring or the disassembly of a castedness change

between the monetary handedness germination
enough when it is not enough to respect the freedom
of ideas but to partake in the possibilities of an
historical grace not knowing ashes equality liberty
such that this is not to insist on a single course and
since progress is only achieved in the dying thinking
that it is useless to debate generations' ▮▮▮▮▮▮▮▮
but that raising children is in itself a form of political
violence aesthetics the reasoning of a community
objection stands or rather sum something together be.

XI
READING TAVIA NYONG'O

Even 'action' seems reduced to the customs of sense in
the manner that affinity is 'conferred by the ways in which
one's spatial coordinates are contested' which as in the
satellite's duress is to be slurred against the string of the
earth's empiricist tongue breadth along and in the
contestation of a hard minoritarian neglect and on and
across as in the Muñozian of what negation in the
exemplary tearoom redoubles from the clear Black trans
rereading of the non-identical where the contestation of
the poem is really just the contestation of the occurrence
of the poem itself and the strength of the entire apparatus
is the strength of the physical symbol system laid out in
its reading as it's located alongside the actuality of writing
and it is the performance of the realism of the world that
acts and things and days where the dead in affinity dense
flourish swerve as in the socio-cognitive which drape and
degrade against the multilinear refinement of the corporeal
which is dying.

XII
PEG AND AWL

[ ]

It's odd to watch against the sentimental valuation of things the
sublime worry over an encounter with beauty or the belief that
there's something like individual experience or progress
in society or art or really any of those things lasting over from
the legacy of the enlightenment which still seems so pervasive
today even despite the better intentions of the eighteenth or
nineteenth centuries which at certain points seemed
to warn against a reliance on the idea of the individual or
the systematic regulation of theory which were all just things
born from the legacy of a singular monotheism or the idea that there
might be some kind of correctness in thinking or the necessity
of symmetry in truth which has stuck around till the present
at least in the history of logic and even the basic idea of ontology itself
is grounded in this way which is all still readily apparent in
so much of moral philosophy like
when people talk about culpability or blame or any kind of intentional
action which of course in reality just takes place against a
background of variable scale and scope and the predeterminants
of previous occurrence and not the absolute given of a sublime or
goodness or effectivity but what's really important here
is that I want these poems to be read without a concern for their
style or message but only for their particular occurrence that

[ ]

which is remarked apart from the material facilitation of the
poems themselves as the desire to resist the naming of
occurrence as amongst a wider set between
the moment of meaning as

the systematic encounter of itself and the singular
interpretation of the poem. That is,
there is a wish to resist the aggregation of a
singular style or voice of the poem despite whatever
or not might be present in the occurrence
of what can be demotically termed 'the meaning
of the poem' which isn't a thing but is already present
before the poem is ever written or read
which just as whatever configuration of the thing
being that which is wider than the poem itself
beyond which the poem is encountered and maintains
framed and unframed
'their works being hidden by the gods' and history
not happening as a way of happening which is to say that
reading is meaningless outside of any social act
and it isn't our knowledge that makes us important but it's
the sum of our works as they are abstracted in the span of our
works and days those being

[ ]

as the undergirding of the poem is not a result of the contemporary
realism of the poem
but that the realism of the poem is the want of the poem
to remember something other than what it is in the artifice of the
poem and not to remember as the distances from the present
          being something
else like now how I'm writing this on my phone
in the dark after staying up worrying about jobs
and money or now as how later I'm revising the poem and
adding to it which has nothing to do with the poem except
that this is the idea of the poem as it exists for me today
which is in contrast to the poems as they rely on a kind of
recognition of the value of their terms or the systems

in other words it's that the only real direction for writing poems
today is to focus on the discursive occurrence of a linear text
and to express contemporary ideas in a clear
and straightforward manner or so as to engage the media form
of the poem and the history of the form in its own function

[ ]

and just as a 'democracy can only describe itself' a part
of what is present in these poems is that there is no
longer the need for any appeal toward a critical
apparatus distinct from the actual experience of a
poem since criticism now can only serve to reenforce now-antiquated
enlightenment conceptions of the progress of
knowledge and human achievement which would say that it might be
possible to gain epistemic insight into things where instead the
                conditions are
actually such that the poem may be encountered apart
from any historically-defined conception of knowledge as
to discard any semblance of a layered or deeper or
veiled meaning as the poem should instead be directed
toward a meaningful intention intelligible to a general
reader and their situation without
the need for any specialised theoretical
knowledge regarding the function of the poetic
apparatus presently at work. It should be understood
that there is nothing more to these poems than that
which is able to be gleaned from a straightforward reading
of the text as it is understood and as it describes itself in reading.

[ ]

I mean, what I'm trying to get at here is that
the directness of these poems is an attempt to avoid the trap of an

enlightenment spectacle of supposed talent or
the modernist veneration of cultural skill
in favour of an egalitarian
of reading where the importance of the poem is conditioned
by the historical setting of what it means for the poem to be read
against the aggregation of the logical ordering of the poem's
form or that there is no
single vector of unequal control in the poem despite the possibility of
degrees or prizes or reputations and that the hope is for the
effacement of a classical picture of beauty or art as to resist the
perfection of heightened speech in the poem instead
relying on the ability of the reader and their situation which
is the frame of the text's judgement. Which is
to say that I hope there is nothing special about these
poems even if that means
that they are not really read or not read in the manner intended
which doesn't matter since I can't say anything about them
that isn't already in the poem or already there
propped up by some invisible grid of thinking
some history of which I am very much ignorant and unaware.

XIII
ELSEWHERE THE

man blinked 'I' 'had' 'gone' 'up' 'stairs' 'to'
'get' 'a' 'book' or the memory of it or which
by the distance within occurs and did
you say it had happened while holding the book
which as the random walk of the thing was
widening of the present in favour of having been
stellen of never not having and can
you imagine not seeing it was at that moment
we had lost or still or it wasn't me but the memory
of did you say which was as with the back

formation of cause and the fervour sternward
dusk affront was not only the secretion of
the idea looking or Minerva's owl or had only
in the realness of some supposed perfection
your seeming in the cryptographic 'same' as
cause or some other kind of hapless giving up.

XIV
STUPID AND ANGER

XV
ACCUMULATION'S LINE

Which in the faculty the Lord our God to parse this
world not ours as body Christ so present single in
the fully formed of will and multiple to God in both
the opposite and not the ebbing light to whom the
simple motion gave ungave which sacraments the
wheel or grid or not disclosed which not as where
we left discern these works and days our purpose not
the fact nor rigour gave critique to answer veil in Glory
give the Lord our God the Temple Shroud which blest
to bless more fully formed itself therein the double
answer dream un-ground to ground critique in rigour
vein forget our own of longing dress as Hopkins'
prevous gainsake nature coming alter subtle born to thee.

XVI

Charcoal grease pencil lacquer etch paraffin leaking the
deflated slick rubber skin shifting in the detailed bloat
of the yellower and smoothing fine wrinkles against the
contorted chest splay bundle of limbs on the sofa crusted

flakes of the rubber his face and breed disfigured carry
forth as the lust dimmed lurch feet metal melted to the
carpet dying on the thick woven circular rope rug as
nylon stockings pressed tight against the shin staggered
up boney to the bent knees where he had been set the
thick curtains' odour heavy smoke and toward the curb
of the street and grass and the rough muscular cracks of
the concrete pavement weeds and rusty chain link there
was no rubbish strewn along only the occurrence that I
am now no longer able to disfigured look you in the face
again.

XVII
AS IN THE HABIT OF A PEASANTRY'S SKIN FADE BENT

o're dour in the conscription bulwark thickening reed
of each in the cancer's will already high in the straw
wove loft as grace dried flower marrow not in dyer's
end which cantilevered shewn and placed and rushed
as dep upon the sun lurched spindle fair lough answer's
wild foxglove burrow nest from distance clip in forth
unrest eternal thee and counterfeit to this to what entail
might still to weepe agoth the blade whose fen plain'd
hill as sop as these not yet the trouble spake contemp.
of verse or how we live or what to do or
rather say in the anthropological saying of how your
will by other people something something Donne.

XVIII
OH LORD THESE PATHS YOUR ARMS

as heaven cloister lone the bars which marked and sprung
and span your wings of we who lost the vigour hope
your gifts your bounty visage gaze WHAT THOUGHTS

I HAVE OF YOU the arc and swell o'er grown whose
lushness font your will intents parse leaves what holds
of common cross to seas our lord our god and father
heaven might that he his only son unbridled greatness
lord you lord who in our deserts guided tilled your
hand give long and spark who less in lines rend drawn
than purpose act abandoned so and lost in world we give
gave back so much in rest so lord give thanks such chain
and land your father's grip be heard and blessèd sallow
give be thus to had this path the way the light the good
thus fury hap to follow skein unwrapped the grip come
trailing strung and wrote your book and line what heavens give
so now you here thus force and low away. The intensities

XIX
DROWNED BOAT

Corroded leech grip arbor mount the clotted dead
which grip block 'camp-ment bed my shoulder
turnt lust finger grief as finger forth the bottom
tug no dear the drowned in boat the dead still
drowned and god still some this deed compound
hum shoulder slumped indeed none circumspect
of knowing shit that death and fear not bowing
place compart these days cast line to drip dawn
bird the lake horizon give and grieve to drawn still
caste sit swatted dusk set sunken flattened hand
survive as life endure the palsy bent of maggots
strewn the five point painted leaf let down fargrgoff.

XX
LORD WHAT DAEMONS DO YOU INVOKE
TO HOUND ME?

How fallow barren wreaths of poems laid and slaughtered
stalk of corpse to think your peaceful son your light the
blood letch God Greek Set mark dwell in things this arc
believe thus dead float oak what shattered fayre had taught
to bind of comlinesses's winter drought and keep with mine
thine fullingnesses' full look back to sheet and gold and steps
tend comfort live and bare what still our dream the Lord
Fortuna bent which Godly what to love in burnished straw
how error thus undo our metric bond to give false bulwark
sovereign grieve bend down in Mithraic vein sprung cock
which let upon this Earth your son and burrow fortune bind.

XXI
END-PIECE

Not buying books in the embroidered edge the
patterned leaves looking gently flora common
lean which in the communal gaud being grieve
midst thick fuck need bereft and curvéd seed
brook dam whyth lace and blister sheath so loved
and stippled crease along cold moulded tore and
lavish hell crypt thick blotch light and stick print
laited over-lain and belly guile as shell reserve
the ridge pearl drip my arc and heart to you thus
walked and forge the lot of sounded let thus see
the colour line of carpet hence the kept of Christ
near fire.

XXII
ALONG THUS SEAM MOVE BLACK BELL BENT

mount oily flanks rise up cut loss production rise
what land sup land lock oil rise sup prairie belt
lock wonder not not food not gone not oil rise
yet rent yon missive thought to sing had valve to
shuck miss firmament seam move black bent
and pollen grace for light and crept stent field glit
rust frack glory winsome garden crank where gold
in rest and weight and berm steep soil rised
that veil bought less in thought than countenance
wan halo's aura pitch let slow in tiled breeze as
steep rough pendent clay half shod half burnt in
green grey rough where midlands dust bowl empty
dawn let dive and drown in oily flank let rise.

XXIII
THE FINALE

Oh acrid Lethe the rank and self regard you hold
leave sodden lust this spate of burnéd drape the
hape and stucco flourid voice. As feignéd anxious
cladding drip flit Merc. crust branch
the tackéd slow of dryad cast still morning line still
fall. Gawk farrow lone the plastic building
drape. How bent and murder left this pass? The flail
clear rent the bodies burnt
the few not home as lone the farrow field the burning
burnt and dead.

XXIV
HOW SAD

Fair in the disappointed gone or having progress
seed in the romantic which even I not being the
kind of fucker which to happen on in the resolute
leniency of mine or the internal slight as this or
in any of the other well respected progressive ways
which at the minute being fair of the aesthetic to
come person being less and gone of the far gram-
matic trundle knowing we this shit as well.

XXV
BRIGHTENED (TO START)

What keep half halt half stern as where aesthetic
heap kern farrow will as pardon sway lap shod fall
star cut stream shut back shear guide seam buck
turn flesh toward strung wrecked now now now
now ashen rod now beauty once but hunger cairn
as beauty hunt and buttress brass burst thing as
first press empty rhizome shuttle no no nothing
no no endless relic nothing thing striation burnt
negation more as ocean's seamless pallet start
where pulpit seam buck mirror whir accord less brief
flut seed.

XXVI
RETROSPECTIVE BELIEF

II.

The romance of self critique is founded thinking something
other than what
to be
or the varied distinction along by which

some other
handedness
between purpose or the appearance of a work
as purpose

might repeated being doing previous
to the encounter
of practice
in the arm's length
contemporary of the poem

which is that which in the appearance of the thing to itself

as in the repeated distance between that doing
and the being previous
to the encounter
remains
the distinction between artifice and the poem
knowing
of the solitary isolation knowing giving memory blame.

XXVII
STARTING AGAIN
'It is both immoral and unfair.'

Deaths enough in the supplicant democratic beloved
falls white sickness grounding fear gird avarice grinding
powder into paste thin skin simply sitting weight atop
bone and the pound blood soaked piss smell blood
issuing of the wretched face pallor sweat hollow when as
Alfred Ross Reggie themselves the grace dug pustules
erring venom as the departed humid night bucolic lethe
which tower grim lock vapour of your body dispel the
democratic too as well of the poor flat blood decision

STET grinding body remand reticence wrapped sallow
gums sunken teeth enlarged in the jewel crust wrapping
laid back being no not for the poverty of crime property
knowing who turned lack nothing else to be but that.

XXVIII
THE GARDEN

Belly cramp bloat assuage of the rope tug corpse
tree sag in its horror frame sits as the loose
skin bonnet apron may or not in the Greek wane
filament of what should be or said written down in
the tear vellum rag preen abstraction turning hung
light of the non-conditional pores filled fatty organs
pustules plastic blood might midnight bloat ill guise
perfect-painéd god to seethe in the gallows poplar
there not knowing the imperfection of knowledge
himself and tried not knowing only to give so long
were given as the long clay Adam preen and breed
set braw of the maelstrom visage might want oh
himself in us and as their desire for an unwanted god
in whose Hill (Golgotha) *rel supplier* revealed himself
to counter in the diagnosis of the fall bodied clothe
still left there hung desiccant follow moisture pestilence
remanding history and the apology of writing debt.

XXIX
PORTABILITY OF STONE ALONG WATER

Unfettered caul seam trans down beyond want
body as alteration's privilege in the light of the
still simple substance of proprietary ease where
the mark of democracy is the ability to change
one's situation however in the wholesale remains

of the stair that no one will climb and I detest
a change in my labour for the benefit of the repeatable
good or to parcel out under the exponential grain
and the board to clarify reflection's critique of the
unendorsed memory which as the rat-catcher's
vice of not wanting as the shoal birch clarity lain
bare to make the crags soiled rock fall to give luster
to your efforts and the sundry ripple down coil neat
thatch to less to fade patched short among the grasses
silence still yet temper guarded previous bleat under
the fallacy of the occurrence experience runs off.

XXX
MY SPEECH IS TO PROVE

Vanity in

and to prove as Sappho's black barbiturate obedience
pruned in the vanity wreck of the supple shoot erection
less than to jut out in the balance pitched seam flower
pressed corpse of the godly immigrant lack what placed
in the sodden preen struggle mask WHO IS TREATING
YOU SO CRUELLY among the dead to raise then bend
vanity the sin is not that as we alive they dead mostly
women and not the rich white men but that their bones
the fruits live on as said the good interred to swallow up
their idle pharaoh saviour dead as much the sin as left
instead the poem of the child's arm linked sodden helpless
drowning bed.

XXXI
ERNST KAPP

1) Equal pay for equal work; 2) Direct
election; 3) Disarm the police; 4) Abol
ition of capital punishment; 5) Wages
are an evil; 6) Free schools supported
by the state; 7) Total separation of mo
ney and state; 8) Total ban on fossil fu
els; 9) Abolition of land ownership; 10)
Aggressive reforestation; 11) Redistrib
ution of private property; 12) Common
allocation of living space; 13) Abolition
of currency; 14) Open all borders; 15)
Everything for everyone without labour
or prejudice.

XXXII
I REFUTE IT THUS

The organ projects what is the true question of poetry.
'If the necessity of every duty is to be estimated by
the frequency with which it is inculcated and the
sanctions by which it is enforced and whose decrees
are established forever in a particular manner the
observation of those commands which seem to be
repeated that they may be strongly impressed and
secured by habitual submission against violation
there is scarcely any virtue we ought more diligently
exercise than that of compassion to the needy and.'

XXXIII
JOY OVER JOY INLAY

Nonconscious bulwark charge of the bulk let sway
grace light press flesh moraine cradle joy over joy

inlay as it is important to remember style being
innocence articulation being genuine hyle layering
not the dream of the crumpled horn cognition where
there's a saying that reaction equal and opposite
furrow corpuscle of the articulation's sway without
grace light press flesh moraine lean harrow dread
now we take the comb from the hive and eat it it is
my body as I am because of you all who beside me
in the occurrence currents of history is to take 'to flee
or move or not, it is all the same; doom is written on
our forehead, it is carried.' Nonconscious bulwark
charge of the bulk let sway grace light flesh moraine.

XXXIV
WINTERS, HOWE, PHILIPS, ALCOCK

I think not in the state nor am concerned with which
way so ever the great helm turned cloth wrung
out in the soft wool left stray slip pilings on the
Brooklyn still tarry flimsy littoral poles where the fairy
remains with its walled up doors wan shapes
eroded sills downstream the strut of the Williamsburg
cable tower as it had thrown its cool
shadow a half a mile inland over the tarpaper
seams gantried water butts splintery tenement
cornices milled with acanthus and classical grasses
of a nineteenth-century dream-slum fantasy why
have one property and not the other is the dilemma
of the loyal dead abolished law goodbye contentment in
goodbye poverty goodbye gross suckling quiet slavery.

XXXV
TRANSUBSTANTIATION (GCC)

Parse any than is weaker faith.

XXXVI
POLITIC OF RIGHT AND STRATAGEM / OF

Right,

Celestial like there are things as such
and more distinct — Hyperion which glare
gave less unto that (Robert) Graves could not
have made some sense of it. Especially, the
third book of which had fallen down into
a darker grace what cast of light and fever'd
hand to keep of writing sequence square of
sink to what some action holds of hand
and our and still and puzzle lest. That we
had any grieve of subtle form and linger
t'ward that stark of pined to wall that did
not wreck some transfer 'pon my thought, had slid
experience nor generous for naught
in alternate of uproar, solemn 'yea.'

Perhaps or not that first break which set ground
to which I owe? Yet we as glisten glean
and honest truth that I attempt yet high
or art in thee avoid of solemn work
and that distinct relief from sense to pass
but none to box or ears or stuff rough-thing
the collar shirt in light. What had of you
expect of such young victim-hood stood right
or care? We overthrow those who keep.
Still I have memory of those things, right?
From the deep sad throat of Melpomene?
As through bronzéd lyre in tragic order go,
and touch the strings to fault a mystery; (which Keats)
who died so perfect faced for lack of love,

that body not so crumpled up as gone,
from sinew which had quickened at his gait
but slant from where? How can I know these things?
That past and not so perfect faced in death
and that the central question: To turn back,
recurse upon yourself, your time, this womb
not splintered over and the like as not.
Which any two still make as sensuous
the meaning then which fall into, of we
to run so present faced into the fray of fire
thus here complete and covered with our text,
thus tracks and marks, thus copper chains of cause,
of motive, means, effect the opposite:
activity constructed by what comes
subjective intervention of none else

         or real.

It is just to be not so twee and all
as like the light at Marlborough. I wake
in morn, my life my own and lean asund'r
ourselves as not. And fine as any sense
may thus pervade, articulate apart
this reach intoward the quiet belt of crit,
as had Avalokiteśvara sat
perfected nihilism of loving grace
or roughed around the forest near for us.
To work against and as hermetic seal
together buffeted and pressed as well
what unguarded recollection we had
in youth that given syntactic agent rest,
on silt-dregged river bottom diction vest.
The character of history is not
so good forget such bound to gods let pray.

XXXVII
######

Gloss: As cocaine blunts along my lady's shallows,
as Donne along the Earl of Essex, rough magic
in this against esteem let write and here abjure.
To bridge to wanter — I on what espied as spritish churl
toward barrow down in listless mar. The thought
had broached my const. appeal, wide reef
my coast who taught to man
what birth in other quarters touch. Apollo,
one of several flounders left to surface die,
per sage who later false had headed see
Bermuda calm. Azores: Rather die a free man
than be enslaved by peace. 'The silver mirrors
catch the bright stones' flare of light and face.' Black
crows in sea foam wantering, weary
('Amphyitryon dedicated me [don't forget]
the spoils of [the rested battle of] Teloboae.').
Yet still, all grace, I couldn't pull a fucking heel.

XXXVIII
THE GOLDEN DREAM

Of humid lapse want blister surface pass and oft.
Buck trundle grieve splint trunk as curve diverg-
ent springtime set point snail rust drip fair acrid
rise strung crest 'Before the Rio-Niterói; Bridge.'
And as not to me to come blue glow to mason
stock sick pine lust glit wave topple hands as ac-
rid lopside table mass move golden wash spec
wrought light sash to bring had brought half glor-
y shadow winsome grieve to sit gave less as
summit fade far future bracket distant palm for
shortened phrase had gone split set slit tower'
d cradle spartan dream stet this and fury transom
something something ending bind.

XXXIX
'LETCH GRIEVE PAPER / DUTY SONULANCE DRIFT'

Uneven ground of the forest floor to rest.
Root barrow river stone
darkening let. Nonesuch else and kept.
Varied masculine instress pulmony wreck.
To this then craft enmeshed; suffering let.
Cleave drop austere sheet drop against;
cord lon down (and aft to lent). Rough
spartan laid in happening yet, quieter breast.
Engrained intoward left tonal spent.
Crush winsom grieve as then to fet.
Impression on
and ration less. Prop days thine own
and laterer lest. Poplar [poplar] afterer

set. Border met. Solemnity, ransom governance
distance sovereignty debt.

XL
SEPULCHRE WRITTEN ON THE OCCASION OF
MY BEING SUCH A TERRIBLE GENIUS

Morn burlap glisten where you of all
after having had —
and as that which much as lighted:

fairness, handedness,
lumpen given —
rivenness of the sore
throat, of rupturing bowel,

slowness linger of the throbbing
kisses, and then
of the then linen lined stained
run lain
burgundy, burgundy,

yellow, damp, urine,
piss,
covered offal in the thin born skin:

GROAN SOARS PISS FUCK GIFTS TO YOU.

XLI
ON TOUCHING THE NECK OF A DEAD BIRD

Flut threat to keep good stature deed still held
yet judge in baited crypt as air now love
as heron death or prev-ous else where blunt

and baited nest — had bolt in bare in life
to death as rock held breast of barren massed
wet earth in spectral yearn wrought wreck as blood
to slit bid stet to say, revise blood's sep-
ulchre to sea too far to Great Neck's granite
vice had writ that after-comers can-
not guess alike the bounty beauty be;
and else as like, as stone what set and nest
upon the hap pass purchase wet, my thought:
as beauty something other happen passion certain
be.

XLII
WATCHING SHADOW FADE LIGHT INTO MARLBOROUGH

Dull nub hot dune clamp and ridden sway

ascent in the numerological
light fades — grip
of the dust foil lamp —
lash of the wood pine recline to lay

as night
bred bare of the this yet yon
divine temperament —
and as your father spurned of the cruelty of the charges
against him —
massive

contoured of the sunken waves — the sun
concave

currencies' of awkward crudenesses, awkward
order of the gravel stung

nowhere — drive
lined veil repeat loath countenanced save
of the wooden house light fade

into Marlborough.

XLIII

same
smae

XLIV
HAD OWED

owns, owned, own, had owned, owning,
holds, held, hold, had held, holding,
is, was, be, had been, being,
has, had, have, had had, having, still

XLV

work working worked laboured labour labouring intend
intending intended wanting want wanted desired desiring
desire assert asserted asserting had asserted intuiting intuit
understood arranged oriented had arranged directed direct
employed employing employ to serve serving articulated
instructed commanded carried argued paid paying

XLVI
TEXTURE WEIGHT RUN HEART STILL LIFE ARCH
BLOOD

As woke far sight out letch mid-winter come;
as rigid nectar hard root shell to back, fate
clasp intoward thus jumble damp bread earth

and crow nut roast meat hew signed leaf
and breadth; and yet, as nature intellect to sway,
to see these things as cause of doldrum ring
engraved, and as Anubis who, in making plain,
what sanctity hold winter trees, 'the sound
your wings,' thin godly crows black fur good
grace to some to smoke dark number organ thrice
a corpse whose centuries not known in gain,
not tansy doublet founding wood, lest vape;
and rush to think foul slender image feel —
as bramble think where I the dead, aft flood
the corpse rest portion sounder pressed;
Hawksmoor the sky our flesh warmed plate
and dipped glint rise sin et / carved out in state.

XLVII

Black godly crows fur hood grain soil vape.

Where Mr. Johnson can't Donne for cause
but nettle-beds and corpse there light
        of darkened rough;
ripe ermine's errant work —
sublation rise methinks these devils be.

Compulsion might as strata
want
and wait to be —

monstrous fatigue.
Metal soft and ward to leave — my writing
changed in meter's key

(empiricist and constant beat,
at best, to bend).

Even worms disgrace whose land addressed
is long but yes:
fatigue.
Lead flower glass, that computation in

and
exponential task
wreath viral load subsist. To me:

Sail corpus blood fuge radic bucket wasteful last.

XLVIII
FAIR LOSS

Redoubled vape of the barren forest rise.
Fold cross in slight rest lacquered seam
set obelisk trees jut memory memorial
metonymy far stars sheet steel shit sky
dusk brightened ease which wrench
resolve of hard cut slight grin hang re-
dundant winter rapture famine sonule
need.

XLIX
REGISTRATE

Lump shit piss govern piss piss govern.

L
REAPED OF SHELTER GIVEN PLUS

Thin godly crows run murder plus
as sounds to wretch alight said flower
lust, which under worn as dark to say
as much as love as vindic gave, blood

marrow Hector Ajax bade which
barrow spake unknowing wind unknown
complex of knowing sigh far down this
corpse bid Paris tend to be, gone dull.

NP, don't you no more no more get dead
on me. And as abeyance naught; worn
under such as which to say, pass weather
ills on nettlebeds, press leaded glass to
save as from the harsher pain, nb: non-
deterministic rigour better longer settle
never wonder ledded harrow this the
thought long linen, leaden, last to be.

LI
IN THE OVERCOMING

Sum wind brocade cross streaked and high bright
plann cool air clipped black lash pine rest arc
dune streak branch low brisk vine sewn gash slump
val hew slit let thine tight trundle river pageant
grieve breast set dismay in slight or less
in stake or stalk [*For Love*] away and tithing lumber
soil pitched long foil form slit back based skull
tráverse still streaming cusp fuck'd retrograde fall
ebullience fay shutt grab stacked lest
streaked or staked or stalked in love
bark black beset befall fall back and place spill
soil ransom other distant
wither single slumber harrow summer hazing rise.

LII

'Woe! Torn down! What value knowing be?'

Pastoral black landscape to name.
Limp branch pin arbor ox wood pine
low woollen thick of love to know
box calculate gone locust thrush
wrench grandeur effort rhizome splint
where valley woe devotion torn
in felis glory long what rest
as pollen garner seed hap stress
of value given bother something know.

LIII

Metallic blaze shim golden bronze blaze
glisten rough pine split hard cut nail
pressed pine tack plate sheet fit cup back
tar keep sand rend sum blaze tuck light
blend keep rise want wrent long look hung
plank pine sheet felt blaze rise up far
knot for grace ground slant land rough grime
far place sheet fit count rend shunt lank
hung crisp tend seamlessness and upwardness
debar.

LIV

Black blackening blackened had blacked
blacked had blackened will have blacked
to blacken to have blacked have to have
blackened blackening will blacken had
blacked will have blackened continued
blackening was blackening have to have
been blackening blackened blacked black

41

LV
IN THE MONOCHROMATIC RIVER'S
LUMINESCENCE ARC TONAL

Hearth metal disk full branch removed in
hull pool tone the water's glist pearl oil slug
tone pattern breach stress glisten oil pearl
outstress branch tone lighght or oil metal
arch glist string rud oil tone blist Richter
oil stress drip oral double ring and pearl
besotted blister pooling ring wet given pearl
glist ring back oil toned and pearling blister
flutter ring.

LVI

Whilst rennet forage
heap knot

   knowing
radix
tangle

in suit or

   follow

   horticulture's

   crystal

   rapid

   crest

glean rise

   solemnity

and shared

   solidity solidity
remain.

LVII

Colors

LVIII
CONTOUR OBSOLESCENCE DERELICTION GAZE

Dep
sun
bridge
set
dune
bough

skim
wrest
glass
stump
pale
black

sill
sheet

wav
set

cloud
long

clear
cis
trench
key
phrase
light

pier
dip
heap
sun
give

LIX
CAREFUL, DON

LUMINESCENCE SONULENCE DEADENING

Baroque lean ark course loft
wood tinder bark press dwell
leaf dusk to low where balanced heart
linch sodden wrenched of inland
oak shit pass lean chord
raised lichen print
and over sodden iris dead
groan cyst heraclitian living rend.

LX
SURFACES

1.

Raise press cause shore lank matter anchor bend

2.

sculpt crass sun vain occasion thing and glor

3.

plate skin fold yearn drift skean and toward

4.

care drift cress give lone blanket poor

5.

raise barely last seam last return unend.

LXI

Potato okra garlic turnip parsnip yam
dill onion cabbage carrot spinach beet
kohlrabi radish mushroom barley hops
alfalfa lettuce chard corn ginger sprouts
gourd apple bean kale rutabaga groat.

LXII
FIELD SCREEN WHAT E

Lang wonder cadence sound thus wreck.
Prick prime dull linger fail to press.
Oft wonder spectre cadence splet.
Thus speech light loss ag fail split ress.
Reign card which wrench faint frame of frail.

Leave link some loss and lumpin cause.
Taught Christ whence furrow frame discard.
Morbidity in cause more sought.
Spoke taut give rise in fainter loss.
Hard rend bank basket farrow ought.
Hap suckle elding parson happen laud.

LXIII
'PRAISE ORIFICE ABSTRACTION NOT KNOWING FADE TIGHT'

As importance without virtue being praise but virtue in
the matter of beauty thought and beauty what as the
reign of knowledge governing in aesthetics as there is no
perfection in knowledge only the enjambment of an
ethical wisdom or falsification of the combine as myth
to nature as the political understanding of the visage
parted curtain curve slight of your naked back shrink
pinkish tonguing back to repeat Lakatos the study
of knowing is as the mind is as of knowing not
knowing place spit come strive divine dire struck not
knowledge in the blister wound pomegranate looking
back in the open mouth wet font of the earth so crystal
enough to save this saying set by saying this the change
as wretched swelling in your body swollen set layering
contrapposto knowing pace Braithwaite in the inhuman
abstraction research program and as here as beauty doth
propose nature then does itself in turn dispose.

LXIV
VERSION 3, EDIT 84

Paste in the cybernetic fog indica score variant
bleat arbor thickening gain. Vex bodies in the

sumpter klaxon whimper. EPAM Accenture
Booz Allen Hamilton Deloitte. Firmament sod
plastic padding tendril drift fence chyron
scuffle. Tubular base
stick bruise fold flex file fix hex com tossing
lasterer. Lossier spun disk blink electric
namesake strata. Heavy daybreak distant
drainage clatter. Gypsum
rock clay tree rota bare breed common wage
decline. Helioscope
thick heap cleat marrow braid frond farrow droop
resign.

LXV

Rough millet stabb pain borrow grief glimpse
sovereign rivet learner stutt. Cut slander glit
bairn chose sheet wince sprain form hiss lumber
hurt. Piss haunted bellow merit sump cept
runner gradual cloven lean. Bulge dock some
corner dwindle pliant flower baseless rend.
Gleam shot luc warren sidelock spect. cede butt
and sewing leather frisk. Stump viral harken
billow rot spine glass shuck proper slant devout.
Shore list move false et grandeur cusp land
glide beige crack change font. Splend eck turn
mond in pound lapse past suck inchoate sumpt
blameless rex and sacerdote divide.

LXVI
IN MEMORY OF OUR SIBLINGS

Right spen vector stoll had callow feet wreck
plain oft dander vale prod forth push grip
sack shod tick lit down gender cank bare sore

spread lip glint blink sat passive hope felt
languid grist balk round stick beat bent
hung as rose as rod as ashen down and groan
shunt supple beam transform of seeing
less and hamper grief give list fet bleed
grope back half hark half beam where long
push creed glint mark path fall steed gape
crank let span to such (to be) confess to
where as whence however wish to live.

LXVII

Ledge plaster wave blot gasp and none striation
said and back. Sunk pathos sounding windswept
barren nighted base recall. Buck land in damp
harsh cramp resolve engrain in tented lamp. Salt
sternward years push linger churlish further rapt.
Split foil thrush wall grist bob glint have hand
give gave give that. Fuse Merc. low tone tank fall
fail set bar pale part lapping past. Damp heron
sunk lent island sand blow rudder standing fete.
Myopic soak hope pleasure blood bleed beaded
tonic lack.

LXVIII
POEM [UNEVEN DISTRIBUTION]

Wretch baited given calm render star stuck
plaster venial Amazon baggies burgeoning
left colour liminal woollen curtains plastic
pink rags wrench cutlery off and orange steno
denim lime crops burn plaid wedge basket
freeze paste blest mendacious rummage
oyster careening velvet fete lumpen wonder

green churning churlish grim cider slat
dexterity coven ancient stairs sans tincture lotus
vacuum spurious glass oxygen curio gain
contrabass set nervous glitter balm slag venom
drip willow pet Sanskrit branch let leotard
glam muffin bent patch corduroy tiny bloom.

LXIX

fine-grain single achieve latencies 10 cycle
performance measure switch tolerate parallel
overhead implementation Encore Multimax
scalability over large-scale describes average
base binary network latency 55 cycles requires
are different uniprocessing parallel environment
machine resident synchronisation the need
add provide other bandwidth processing exploit.

LXX
ABOUT POETRY TODAY

ABOUT POETRY TODAY

Nothing anybody can say is going to apply to all of poetry
today.
Except maybe saying that it *is* 'poetry today'
or at least maybe something like
'poetry in the near present.' I mean,
it is difficult to try to say anything, but

there's something very personal about pretending
to be able to talk about
the entirety of poetry today as if such singular a thing were to exist.
There's something very personal about talking
about it.

The personal experience of saying something about the present
is a very conceptual thing.

LXXI
'Forme of speche is chaunge.'
THE DIFFICULTY

of reading comes in the lack of methodological specificity offered
by the poem not giving to the interpretive or moral imperative
put forward by the poem which is to say that in any case the real
argument of the poem is in the forgetting of one line to the next
or in the enumeration of certain terms through which the sense
of the poem already remains elsewhere extending beyond a
commonly agreed upon empirical perception 'and I was thinking
about the many people who said' which is the seamlessness of a
cultural memory and perception of as to say I'm sweating a lot
by now which in the argument of the poem is really just the repeated

contradiction of the poem which is repeated like how the poem
repeats things you might have already heard or that this poem has
already contradicted itself in making an argument but I can't even
really understand what it is leaning on the door of the john whispering
breathless or gasping or whatever *New World Writing* or not.

LXXII
WHICH IN THE VARIED CLASS OF
METHODOLOGICAL APPROACHES AVAILABLE

to the poem being the literalness of abstraction and to be
read against the history of the monetisation of rent or the
long shadow of the parliamentary vote which in the aesthetic
of the poem is as the ecstatic shape of the firebombed house
or the symbolic plowing of a truck into a busy sidewalk or
the directness of violence being not for the sake edification
but for the closing of the somatic veil of our experience and
not abstraction which wedded to the selling of exchange
as knowing that the action of the past cannot be undone
even if by a monied class who themselves are brought up
knowing the skills of intimidation and violence and inherited
wealth and whom I would dearly wish die or be killed in the
civility of an unrequited patriotism such that my children
might be better pleased to live under the total collapse of
nature knowing that everything that might had been done
had not failed ourselves to them whose works and days and
grief upon grief of betters' nature auguries shape and theirs.

LXXIII
OR AS TO SAY IN THE NOMINATIVE DISTINCTION
BETWEEN IDEAS

and things or words and the difficulty of 'la petite' being
the misunderstanding of the value of expression in that

there's no value in expression except for the lack of beauty
being the circumstance of writing just as reading is not
enough for the concerns of the poem which just like how
the political problem of class is itself rarely meaningful
outside of the political problem of class itself except in
the vanity of thinking as experience is only coherent to
an understanding of individuated action and not the
formation of a perspective to set up among the world or
the rationalism of some coded grid like the brutalism of
my table pressing against the concrete floor of your room
at night when it's dark and everyone else is asleep and I

LXXIV

'possession mocks desire'
ON THE OTHER HAND MY

general complaint about ▮▮▮▮▮▮▮▮▮ is that it repeats certain
ideals and forms which support the reproduction of the property
rights of those individuals who in their historic connection to
centres of cultural and economic power are able to utilise the
claim that there might be something like progress in the arts in
order to maintain an ownership over others ignoring the historical
racial and economic constitution of categories like culture or
language or race or even the foundational valuations of the
supposed ahistorical mandate of occurrence or criticism or that
the recognition of the repeatability of reading and not writing
is in the contrasts of a more scientific against the individuation
of objects which are really only located within some particular
constellation of effect and individual desire which is all to say
that ▮▮▮▮▮▮ works are only maintained in the crystalline
repetition of the will of a privileged class where the purity of
desire is held as the bulwark of statist violence and veridiction
being the ability to resist critique left alone to play at being aesthetic
martyrs to their own intelligence and to arbitrate the guarantee

that they will not die in the gutter for want of food or a terrible disease or more probably that someone else will be killed by the police for not acting in accord with the purity of some concept. We

LXXV
AND YOU HAVE TO UNDERSTAND THAT IN THE PROCESS OF READING

any theory of reading or the idea of ontology or aesthetic theory is just *another* appendage to the poem like right now how there's a conviction that one line follows after the next and there's something like the idea of ordering or like in the case of criticism or aesthetics how they're all connected to things like friendship or knowing or different attitudes about writing which is just that there is so much outside of the poem that's not explicitly part of it like factories or farm workers or processor fabs or like how someone might say something to you when you're in line at the grocery store or it's like when you see something in the news or read it in *Frieze* that week and there's a point when you have to make decisions about individuation and cause and believing that one thing might be different from another and that *that* decision is all part of the work as well and not necessarily in any recursive or intrinsic way but that the possibility to recognise something as a poem is only a loosely defined concept that's changeable but nevertheless it's the same as anything else except that it's different in some way and just happens to be what we're paying attention to right now or something like that or whatever.

LXXVI
WHICH IS TO SAY THAT WRITING IS ONLY EVER A RE-ARTICULATION OF SOME

previous state of affairs and I can't really say anything
else except that reading is also a kind of re-articu-
lation and that to be able to say anything about writing
or especially to be able to recognise that some writing

might be poetry or art and others not it's that you have
to rely on a specific kind of knowledge or habituation
about writing or art and there are some things you can
just pick up or piece together but really writing is a kind
reading that folds back on itself and there's no progress
in anything except in the way that reading gets re-habit-
uated over and over again and that there are certain

[epistemic] privileges given over to reading or at least to
certain kinds of reading which are held apart and managed
like how so many kinds of reading are linked to the idea
of progress or the explicit critical annunciation of value or
the founding moment of an author's intent or the claim
that there's some transcendence in the development of
form which in the thimblerig of saying that all art after
Duchamp is conceptual is only to shift the ground of
criticism away from form and toward intent which as a
sacrament of belief might just be something talked about
between friends or written down in passing which in any
case is simply a matter of the annunciation of some aesthetic

§

which is a tough claim to pretend when the form of a work
is proximate to the text itself as the reader can only be
told about the form of a poem by the poem itself and
anything else is just a misunderstanding of how culture or
communication is always just built out of our own repeated
gestures of appropriation and that language and ideas are
only ever language and ideas in that they're only ever embed-
ded and reproduced as part of wider systems like history or
the reproduction of organic forms or whatever else there is
in the history of our own intelligibility or the coding and de-

coding of things which is nothing other than a recognition
of the fact of metaphysics which is just the name of something

which is given to the ability to recognise certain ideas or
systems of cause or the various components of language as
they put description into relationship with other things or locates
them along a field of occurrence and it's funny to see arguments
made against expression when every laying out of language
happens in the same way which if it weren't for their moral
anaemia or bigoted love of a great man theory of history would
be funny since there are so many who are so classically expressive
in their views about writing or not writing that it's easy to fall
back into what is an exceedingly traditional perspective since

language or culture is always just the rearticulation of some
previous state of affairs and really it's that the idea of advancement
or progress is itself really uninteresting in that it is exactly what
everyone has been up to this whole time anyway no matter how
they talk about it it's just the way things are done in language or
culture or whatever which is to say that things have always been
different from one moment to the next or as ideas move from
one line to the next just like right now except that the claim of
advancement is the only genuinely repetitious and dull kind of
expression which as a veil between the artist and the work is
what poetry has always been up to since Plato at least in the
setting up of the artifice and the moment of saying 'this is not

§

what it appears to be but something else' but for the life of me
I can't think of what deskilling in writing might look like since
even the repetition of language involves the skilful negotiation
of some context which is the whole point of language or the
legitimation of code but it's an interesting question and not

surprising that some people might want to think about how it's
possible to differentiate among various kinds of repetition
even as they may not want to worry about race or cultural or
political infrastructure but you can't really be interested in
repetition without thinking about culture or the history of
things since ideas of individuation or cause or the possibility
of recognition all rely on the present and not just the supposed

singularity of the intention of repetition which in any case is
very explicitly a matter of identity and never of the work itself
except as the work exists alongside its happening where the
intention of the artist and their specific cultural identity is
embedded within a wider sphere alongside the work as it re-
articulates some previous state of affairs in its gesture which
might be the assignation of authorship or the claim of
intention except it's the repetition of gesture or the recognisable
idea of the possibility of the repetition of any gesture that
confounds the possibility of intent where the idea is already
distinct from anything in the present and itself as it's
against the solidity of form or the lastingness and what I want
to get at here is that the repetition of language or writing is
never repetition and that things are always changing and that
it's the speculative intention of the supposed novelty of the work
rather than the wider integration of the occurrence that
comes off as repetition or the closing off of one unit from the

next which just goes to show the asymmetry that's at play in the
social framing of repetition or of the work in general as it pushes
against the intentional setting of a supposed present and the
point is that it is the perseverance of the present that is needed
for reading or the repetition of writing or a sensible account
of any of mode of writing as intention is always co-equal
with movements of state violence and that the mores of the
deontological judgement of writing or the labor of reading are

only 'mores as in mores of the State' which to speak more
specifically here in ending are enacted via the apparatuses of
public things like funding bodies and institutions all of which
are part of the intentional framing of the thing inside the
public realities of the work which privilege the idea private
property or intention or an opposition to unionisation which
is itself the codification of happening against intention and
I'm not sure if I believe in any of this or its opposite since
after all any person can just as easily be replaced with another
just like how anything can be easily changed depending on
its degree or context or where it stops or is made to end.

LXXVII
'AS COMES WITH THE BODY NOT FREELY GIVEN'

Where the movement of the body being as a positivism without belief
being empty.

As the poem within the academy is to have already
been done

which as a positivism without belief being empty

and as the other meaning of the poem not given
except in the movement of the body reading

which is in the decision or not to read
or not in the belief that you

not reading as the insistence of not reading or more
often than not the assertion

of not except in the movement of the body
which is reading

which as a positivism without belief being empty.

The repeatability of reading and not writing being
the positioning of the body.

The poem being the naturalisation of the body
to reading.

The position of your body as that to fit to some other
position being desire.

LXXVIII
'. . . allows, participates, loves.'
THE CONCEPT OF FREEDOM IS SUCH THAT YOU CAN'T

worry about intention or what to do or the meaning of the
thing and it's only in the repetition of history that the moral
culpability of a legalistic or punitive framework appears which
is to say that practically speaking I'm more concerned with
whether or not I might need to go to the shop to get some
milk for my kids or whether somebody needs new shoes or
why the fuck housing costs just keep rising all of which
seem to be more pressing right now than the good grace of
a moralistic purity or arguments about epistemic validity
which in the prosody of a certain Polish poet's poems just
seem to be an apology for the accumulation of capital by
which I mean that the world will just go on either way so
maybe everything just happens and events are set up to
demonstrate the repeatability of the repetition of events
and maybe that's not correct and there's a real and pressing
need for us to think about the choices we make in an abstract
way as they fit within a wider field of sociological effect. Or what.

LXXIX
'I NEVER HAD ANY IDEAS'

except that the reality of deskilling in the arts extends the
shift of the site of virtuosity away from the ability of a vis-
ceral reproduction of the classical line to the development
of organisational [or socio-technical] tools such that there
is a reduction of the overall capacity for critique outside of
the terms established by the work with all this being founded
on an avant-garde hostility to pre-capitalist considerations
of art and this isn't at all meant to support a defence of
tradition over other kinds of deference but just that the
confines of the privilege of judgement remains active in both
conservative and radical incidents of the will however cut
which is to say that no matter the intent any idea of meaning
or cause whether before or during is as suspect as any other
with the one bright spot being that for once this sad state isn't
solely the result of the press of the market [meaning that
arguments around rationing can be overcome] but instead relies
on the tacit belief in the divine grace or the ability to forecast
the fetish myth of unlimited growth which isn't true anyway
but really the point is that critique faces a challenge as
works no longer exist within a restricted economy but circulate
among a wider and continually interdependent system of effects.

LXXX
REALLY IT'S THAT THERE'S NO WAY TO JUDGE
THE QUALITY OF A

poem besides the critique presented by the poem itself or it's that
the critical gaze invited by the poem is dependant on the scale
at which it is read or the way in which the poem presents some
depth of field to the reader and it's like the way that you worry
about word choice or the specificity with which the poem moves

'but ha (ha*ha*)' none of that really matters and unlike the shape of the poem or the kinds of things that get talked about in the poem and a lot of the time you can just look at a poem and know whether it's any good or not without actually reading it which is nice and this is something different than thinking about artifice or the material accumulation of the poem but I mean everyone's situation is different and you can always just think about something else if you want like Jacqueline Humphries' wonderful black lights and how there's no progress in painting except maybe for her at the moment but really it's just about about how the poem is right here with us in the present or that really 'this is the only language you understand, ass-face!'

WHICH AS A QUESTION OF PLEASURE POETRY IS A VERY PERSONAL THING

and any decision or question about poetry is in the end a
very personal thing since it's about pleasure and there are
all kinds of pleasure in poetry like the pleasure of listening
to the sound of the waves lifting rocks from the shore and
having them drawn out by the current and then dropped
down in a clatter as the froth recedes and this being the kind
of thing that people usually think about when they think
about the pleasure of poetry or tranquility or the sublime
eloquence of the articulation all of which we know isn't

really anything other than a habit that's instilled as a

kind of cultural memory of how to think about poetry but
what's important is that even knowing that it is a kind of habit
that's learned it's still possible to enjoy the revery of a poem
and to play along anyway just for the fun of it or it's like the
way that these common threads of pleasure that we can
identify in a poem make it easier to share things with other
people or to have a conversation about a poem since you don't
have to think or worry as much about what someone might
expect from a poem which makes it easier since everybody
already has an idea of what kind of pleasure might be expected
in a poem or it's that we can have an idea of what kinds of
pleasure readers might be interested in when they read a poem
which is important since it's not a poem without pleasure but

what's really key here is the variety of pleasure possible in a

poem just like love or sex or pissing or like how throwing a street
sign through a car window can be pleasurable or how hearing

about landlords getting dragged out and beat up reminds
us that other forms of social relationships might be possible
which is like the pleasure of a poem as it changes or makes
things happen in our relationships and it's a pity that so many
of our things today are monuments to control and accumulation
since a lot of the time the pleasure of poetry is the same as the
pleasure of fucking or to anarrange[1] social discourses or histories

or really all of which is the lineage of the work of differentiation

and sameness or to take an early interlude and to point out the
explicit approach being taken here which is that there's a
reflexivity to all this and I'm trying to be conversational about
things and to avoid the overbearing tendencies of so many
hybrid texts like in the case of you-know-who or even you-
know-who-else both of whom produce great work but it's just
that there's a need for a discussion which is less tied to any
specific poetic or academic lineage and is instead more like the
thing that Baldwin points to when he talks about those lost
expatriates in Paris who seemed to be there 'to pursue some
end, mysterious and largely inarticulate, arbitrarily summed up
in the verb *to study*'[2] which I can only think without checking is
where Moten and Harney[3] got their use of the term but whatever
the case it's that the enrolment or historical trajectory of the
poem or the assembled vector of travel of the poem is for me
an argument that works both for and against arguments about

---

1   As from Fred Moten's 'come on, get it!' from *All That Beauty*
(2019, p. 19). It is also found elsewhere in Moten's work such as Moten, F.
(2013) 'Jurisgenerative grammar (for alto)', in G. Lewis and B. Piekut (eds)
The Oxford Handbook of Critical Improvisation Studies. Oxford, UK: Oxford
University Press (Oxford Handbooks), pp. 128–143.
2   Baldwin, J. (2012 [1955]) 'A question of identity', in *Notes of a
Native Son*. Boston, MA: Beacon Press, p. 128.
3   Harney, S. and Moten, F. (2013) *The Undercommons: Fugitive Plan-
ning and Black Study*. Brooklyn, NY: Minor Compositions.

the formal qualities of a poem or its being-ness in that the
poem is always situated in so many ways as is the living and
continually existent core of the poem or the material occurrence
of it which is as always being read or the retreading of the
ground in reading which is always just about getting it wrong
especially when you're thinking about art and error or the
differentiation of things which exists previous to the possibility of
truth which is that there's no immediate virtue in saying anything
which is such an old story that it doesn't really have any value
either except that it's wrong to intimate that there's anything
except the idea of value which reminds me of a riddle one of my
kids told me once which asked 'what's something that one person
has that another person wants?' the solution of course being 'the answer
to this riddle' which is to say that any response is unable to be

thought outside of the frame structured by the joke and really

it's that cultural critique or any kind of cultural activity like a
poem always exists within some previous form or idea of what
can be pleasurable or not which is to wonder about how maybe
we should just allow certain things to be forgotten or to maybe
just ignore things and to let whatever we don't want around
to just fade away since there's that kind of coupling that exists
between things whatever's being said about them but the truth
is that there's still an acting upon which lasts over forgetting
like how institutions or paperwork or algorithms or ideas about
poetry act without thinking and how we should maybe reconsider
the idea of social forms in a way that isn't focused on a progressive
reading of history and that social change or change in the arts
doesn't occur in an evolutionary way or as an overcoming of bad
ideas by some better ones but really it's that the social or cultural
organism is just a monolithic thing which exists only just as it is
with all its various parts and regions being component of the same

thing which is really just itself pocked with the wear of time and language where the interdependent organs of differentiated or regionalised culture are incidental to value or pleasure and aren't rendered through an evolutionary or even bodily process or overcoming which is to say that human culture is really nothing other

than a continual occurrence and not the progressive accumulation

of knowledge or experience or which is to say that there's no root to the idea of experience other than its own occurrence being something like sameness and maybe there's no such thing as a change in culture or that any ideas about the differentiation of culture are just rooted in a kind of racist or parochial notion of uneven differentiation or like how Moten puts it when he says that '[t]he idea of the avant-garde is embedded in a theory of history. [A] particular geographical ideology, a geographical-racial or racist unconscious, marks and is the problematic out of which or against the backdrop of which the idea of the avant-garde emerges. The specter of Hegel reigns over and animates this constellation'[4] and while Moten might be talking specifically about the avant-garde this really goes for thinking about history or culture in general and how there's no such thing as social progress except as an ideological

program which is to say that social or cultural forms don't develop

in an ordered or orderly fashion but are just a series of rearticulations held over from one moment to the next [one line to the next] and like I said it's not about the compounding of experience but about the differentiating and re-edification of the occurrence

4   Moten, F. (2003) *In The Break: The Aesthetics Of The Black Radical Tradition*. Minneapolis, MN: University of Minnesota Press, p. 31.

of a material cultural habit which in any case is outside of experience or nature and what's important is that differentiation isn't piecemeal or particulate but like I said the process of cultural development is previous to the idea of nature which just as localisation is the time it takes to recognise what might be present it's individuals and generations which are not reducible to biological or cognitive causes but exist within a wider field of the pre-natural and irreducible differentiation which is to wonder if there's space within this to think about individuals or presence or the idea of action or even to differentiate specific cultural groupings or

regions from anything but 'study' nevertheless exists only in this

moment of you reading this now and I am also reading the words here at this very moment which is not a separate time since it's located here in this poem and like how Nicole Brossard said the poem is 'always in the present when you're reading it, and when you write it'[5] and you have to remember that I'm trying to read in a way that is intelligible or pleasurable to you and that there *is* some possibility for communication or a communal pleasure or even the demarcation of empirical knowledge which is laid across the wideness of structure and even in the heroic uses of study like in Baldwin or Moten it remains fitted within the prescribed estuaries of relation and knowledge and change all wrapped up in the academy of publishing where even within this the individual

of recognition or naming is just a version of Cartesian doubt

but where madness is a question of social intelligibility instead

5   From an interview conducted by Catherine Mavrikakis found in Brossard, N. (2020) *Avant Desire: A Nicole Brossard Reader: A Nicole Brossard Reader*. Edited by S. Queryas, G. Robichaud, and E. Wunker. Toronto, CA: Coach House Books.

of cognition and it's like how Duchamp said[6] that he liked
Warhol's paintings since you didn't really need to look at them
which to me isn't really about the fact of not looking or the
concept or the move away from the retinal image but is
about the tacit knowledge that's involved in understanding
works of art and how the thing of the work facilitates social
interaction which is to know that there is something there to
look at or not or to think about or that they are connected
to wider social and historical movements and aesthetics or
whatever and it's that a bunch of things are communicated
previous to anything or not communicated and really are
just simply already the case and this is important for poetry
since you have to be able to recognise that something's a poem
to get certain kinds of pleasure out of it or at least to get the
kind of pleasure you'd expect with a poem which is a really
diverse thing since poems don't need to be read in any partic-
ular way but there is an epistemic required in the veridiction

of a poem or knowing that something is a poem as it exists with

in a wider social totality and it's important to know the difference
between solidarity and vanguardism or the reflection of the
differences in the pleasure of the thing which is really and most
acutely about the possibility of the differences in the pleasures
of things since that's all we can really think about since we don't
know anything about a poem except the pleasure that we get
from reading it and there's something silly about domestic metaphors
of pleasure or the sensuality of the poem like talking about ink or
perfume or the texture of a page all of which are nice things
but really don't have any bearing on the metaphysics or the not-

6   As Duchamp put it in 1965: 'If you take a Campbell soup can and
repeat it 50 times, you are not interested in the retinal image. What interests
you is that concept that wants to put 50 Campbell soup cans on a canvas.'

metaphysics of the encounter with a poem except in the way

that all things do and I would rather just talk about whether I have
an upset stomach or how I feel mad when I don't have enough
time to write or how work sucks or maybe that it's such a beautiful
day or the great feeling I get when I think about free and federated
software or healthcare but really there's a great resilience to being
open to disagreement like how Moten and Harney welcome the
resistance to the idea of study into the idea of study itself saying
that 'it's also fine for people not to use it or to find something else.
But, equally, I think that the point about study is that intellectual
life is already at work around us . . . cut through in different kinds
of ways and in different spaces and times'[7] which is a nice illustration
of how to work against the idea of form and to allow occurrence

to configure itself in whatever way but I guess that the point I
want to make is about the way that structure or form 'gradually
develops out of successive contributions from a number of
component instincts'[8] which is Freud talking about sexual urge

but the idea is the same in that the recognition of figures or the

identification of the bounds of differentiation which is the over-
lapping figure of an object and understanding which is always
in the pleating over and rearticulation which is like the always
multiple of experience and like how in Husserl there is still the
collocation of horizons which only really exist in the anticipation
of some non-present which is the abstraction of auto-affection
where it's not such a simple thing to be able to work backward
toward or to be able to get to any final root of of some idea or

7   From their interview with Stevphen Shukaitis in *The Undercommons*.
8   From *An Outline of Psychoanalysis*.

at least that's what I got out of Len Lawlor's lectures when I was at Penn State[9] and really there's a broader issue with trying to engage with classical metaphysics or really that it's tough to talk about surplus since any surplus is just the basis for some further-ance which is not surplus but simply the state of things as they are which is the lesson of form or the figure as they are only those things here with us in the present or the near present as we have been given and recognising delineation or calling out something by its name is our problem in trying to talk about form is that it rests on an understanding of form to begin with and poems

aren't about form but are about pleasure and to really try to say

anything else other than in an oblique way is either kind of foolish or maybe just pig-headed and when I first read *All that Beauty* I was really confused by Moten stretching the text across the broad width of the page and how that made it so tough to read except it's so great when you go back and look at the lineation of the earlier Belladonna* version[10] of some of it and you can see how the length of the line is determined by the width of the available page and it's about the different forms that the poem takes given the situation or the publisher which is the lesson like when Jeremy Toussaint-Baptiste was talking about the possibility of a baseline in painting and sound in that '[a] new world can't look like what we've seen; it can't sound like what we've heard, and it can't feel like what we've felt before. . . . [T]here is no way of denying that

9   See Lawlor, L. (2012) *Early Twentieth-century Continental Philosophy.* Indiana University Press; Lawlor, L. (2016) *From Violence to Speaking Out: Apocalypse and Expression in Foucault, Derrida and Deleuze.* Edinburgh University Press; and Derrida, J. (2011) *Voice and phenomenon: Introduction to the problem of the sign in Husserl's phenomenology.* Translated by L. Lawlor. Evanston, IL: Northwestern University Press.
10   Belladonna* chaplet number 218, *from* Day (Moten, 2017)

the ground is still the ground'[11] which is nothing to the issue of
form no matter what we might want there's nothing to do even if
we say 'fuck form' and do something else instead since there's
always an elsewhere to the ground of the situation of our speaking
which is the fact of form in poetry and pleasure pleasure being
the through line of the argument of the poem which is in the end

just the rearticulation of form.

11   From Samantha Ozer's interview with him in *Art Forum*, August
31, 2020. Elsewhere, Toussaint-Baptiste makes specific reference to Moten
and Harney ('Jeremy Toussaint-Baptiste in Conversation with Nicole Kaack'
in *Sound American*)

ALL THOSE DIFFERENT MONISM

'If chance will have me king, why, chance may crown me without my stir.'

1

And the argument here is that the poem offers a reconfiguration

of the field of meaning extending backwards so that any
subsequent evaluation is always predicated on something
previous and it's like how today we're not so
worried about what Plato said but it's that we're worried
about how we understand Plato today or I mean this isn't
really about Plato or about how we understand Plato but
really it's about Anaximander or Heraclitus or maybe the fact
is is that the poem isn't really going to be about today or
about what's 'going on' or anything like that and anyway
it's probably just about immediacy and the present and
thinking about cause and the idea of a backwards
reconfiguration and this isn't just the case with poems but
is actually the case across the whole of occurrence and
it's that the semblance given by the poem isn't just inter-
pretive or only about the poem or the meaning of the
poem but is actually just like everything else and is
about the reconstitution of a material history or the
effects of history and the material of the thing and maybe

2

the poem is only such that it serves as a surface between

actuality and the ideal and I mean that's if there really is
even anything like the ideal and not just the thought
of the ideal but in any case it's that the poem is always
right here with us like in the way that the shapes of the
letters absorb light or reflect and it's that reading opens up
a kind of virtuality in appearance and tells us something
in a mechanical kind of way which in the extending

reach of things and it's that right now I'm thinking about
word processors and networks and computers which
is to say that this is all about infrastructures of writing
and maybe it's the same for any system like language
or genetics and that there's something there which is the
conveyance but it's important to understand that any
coded system is always about the simultaneity of reading
and writing which are not really differentiated by anything
other than their occurrence in the present which in the case

3

of the poem is to wedge itself between the existing or as a

negation of any dialectic of matter and form and you have
to keep in mind that outside of a bounded system there is no
such thing as entropy and that there is always an elsewhere
to occurrence or some kind of conjunction or coupling which
in the overlaps and delays of sense or of what is the over-
lapping of sense being the accumulation of the assumption
that there's a single pointed arrow to time or a flatness to
things or a homogeneity to cause which is the otherwise of
recognition and maybe we should just think about change in
a different way or maybe it's all about the transubstantiation

4

of the idea of change which I guess is in the remembering

of one line to the next and the poem is never empirically
present except to yourself and to the ballast of sense as one
moment to the next and across and just as the general and
not in the particular picture of a reduction of sense being
each of which are the same as the largest of to mat down
the specificity of our renderings is just foolishness in the
texture and occurrence of the thing or the striation and

as striation's vector and compositing distance to be and
everything and I'm sitting here looking at the floor and all
the jagged lines of the planks running along the length of
the room and they're splintering and the dark varnish and
knots and textures against the brown and the uneven way
the planks join up all of which is the horizon of intelligibility

5

and as the instress of the wood itself or I mean it's that in

any observation there's the tacit knowledge of each particle
of the wooden plank and the state of the wood and the
specific mass and position or the distribution of charge which
as the unknowing of the distance between each observation
being the establishment for the conditions of change to be
noticed and the difficulty of simultaneity is trying to look
across the distance of any observation and to think about
cause and the supposed discontinuities of any non-determinist
frame or the muddle of effect and in the case of the wood
it's the suddenness of the expression of the board in any
empiricist account of the form and the frame and how the
field of experience comes into contact with the field of the
wood and the simultaneity of difference and detail and
there's an impossibility of 'knowing' in the occurrence of
the plank as it's stood upon or an unimportance of some
kind of perfected knowledge of the condition of the wood
or like the way that the wood has been logged and milled
and stacked up and how each tree had been grown and its
own particular distance from the sun and the atmosphere
and air currents or the nutritional composition of all those
individual grains of topsoil or it's the way that all the various
molecules of seeds being sloughed off as it grows and how
the pathways and root structures of nearby trees pressing

6

in and the solidity of things and density which as the cause

of the tree is in the foundry or the mill and in the stamping
out of the saw blade and the tempering and the boots of the
loggers and the trucks and corporations and monetary
systems and the history of their genes pumping blood and
breathing in the solid sea of air and moving and needing
in the participation of ownership and land rights and what-
ever the circulations of capital which in the history of it
comes as the a priori condition for knowledge which as
the recollection of pure forms and the causes of form and
the function of seeing or the evolutionary pathways of like
how it is with the land rising up or the affordance of the
thing or being able to think about cause or the foundering
of social organisation among the local community and the
possibility of the loggers enjoying their labor and maybe the
worry about tree spiking and how someone somewhere had
read about monkey-wrenching in a magazine or heard about
it from a friend or the wider history of the tradition of direct
action and there's something about how we use wood in
construction but maybe it's more just about clearing land for
grazing and the market structures of profitability than any actual

7

uses of lumber really but the variousness of cause and the multi-

plicity in which computation relies on the exponential of branes
and branes built up and within and across which is to say
that cause is not a simple thing or any as singular as the inter-
section of one plane along another in empty space but it's
about the manifold of the entirety of the (localised) area of
effect which as an informational resource relies on the fact
of someone caring or that there are those things which are

attended too like the day's duties or the drunken dumbshow
which is that it's appropriate that there are such things as will
or the development of something called will which even as set
within the wider concerns of the climate and even apart from
purpose and how you can think about the slow growth of trees
over years and layers and everything brushing against the bark
and the air and moisture and the molecules of CO_2 moving in
and out of the tree in the permeability of the branch and
mapping out the structure of the roots and deposits of salts and
alkalies and what had happened to the soil years ago and is
still happening as in the futurity of cause which is change and
the unmoving passage of time and it's that cause is not at all

8

specific like in the sequential rearrangement of atoms and it's

that in writing the poem I have to wonder how we can talk
about something like the texture when there's no bottom to the
idea or of the way that two points might be thought to differ
in which the reality of the difference is reduced to the subjectivity
of the sensing subject like how poetic meter falls amongst the
granularity of understanding or the multiplicity of possible
meters as actuality is the stack or scale of each moment
being the chance which time takes or several in being seen
or accounted and it's the repeating movements of distention
or condensation and as the cadence of belief in currencies
or speculative markets and maybe there is a benefit to just
having an encrypted string of digits which is not about any
kind of intrinsic investment but about the verification of some
manifold of H-Space as it locks in a specific observation and
either or the possibility of a non-statistical aggregation of
virtuality which is to say that cryptography can be leveraged
in opposition to probability which just as currency has always
been about the facilitation of the certainty of the movement

of goods or I guess what I'm talking about here is the reification
of the movement of the will and that if it's to rely on the time
that computing takes as cause and it's the arbitrary distinction of
cause and the accounting of the chain of effect which is as the

9

ungrounding of phronesis and I guess we're maybe more naive

than we'd like to think and maybe the point of the destruction
of philosophy is that value or judgement or whatever is always
just a question of the exactly same and you can draw a line
from that back to Plato or it's just like the way that Heidegger's
existentialism is not a humanism in that it thinks being beyond
some set of principles except that it's still dragged down into
the aperture of phenomena which in the present day is more
about the relation of the human being to the world or I mean
it's just another tugging at a kind of substance and maybe this
is all just about Meno's question and the definition of justice
or maybe more about the way that Socrates worried about
definitions or I mean Plato which all feels a little redundant
today since we all know how definitions are supposed to work
except that maybe the Greeks weren't actually worried about
any definition in a positivist sense but only in the phronesis of
the social interaction of the definition but in any event maybe
that's the point anyway since our understandings of definitions
these days aren't wedded to any kind of logical specificity or in
the delineation of any essential characteristics but are just thought
of as networks or contexts or clusters of things which allow us
to make some claims about a specific regionality of the world and
that that kind of condensation of things is more than a little

10

problematic in and of itself like Plato's ideas about pure forms or

the repetition of those ideas which in either case involves a volition
toward the possibility of the definition or at least the specific
willingness toward an epistemic intervention on behalf of the
idea and to bed down in the sync of logic is like falling asleep
in the warm purity of snow or forgetting of the Lethe in death
but the political legacy of univocity is that caring people are
relied upon to be the advocates for some kind of classical
liberalism and the singleness of identification is that it's the
responsibility of rational people and it's like how maybe
it's the duty of practical or caring people to advocate for
some kind of classical liberalism which is really just their
wanting to live well but it's pretty clear that it's a drag to
have to worry about other people all the time or to worry
about how they understand the world which is like a
generational thing or a drift in ideas themselves and there's
a degradation or distortion over time or I mean it's like
how liberalism or even morality isn't a mathematical
concept or anything that can be easily stated or inputted but

11

it's that the purity of the thing is wrecked by the belief in

the outside or of the volitional acceptance of some terms
not immediately present which is just common sense I guess
or I mean that when we start to point elsewhere or to hold
some belief it is that we always have to point elsewhere for
definitions which is about the lack of certainty like in the
case of things like crypto or speculative markets or anything
that's not present or I mean anything that's not an a priori
fact but a kind of mechanical configuration that one thing
has to rely on the next in some fashion and you know I

just have to stick in here that I'm not committed to the concept
that there's only a finite set of physical dimensions to things
which is to say that there's more to the idea of a dimensional
space in the way that things hang together which is a totally
post-monist kind of way to think about it particularly in that
intelligibility requires the overlay of measurements onto our
ideal of dimensionality or subjectivity and the demarcation or
relativity of change being necessary for the ongoing calculation
of occurrence and I guess this is the point where I want to

12

imagine mathematics without the possibility of zero which

is really just about the question of the structural dependencies
of a null state and I can't imagine the reality of anything like
zero without relying on some kind of artifice and I always think
about the medieval prohibition against debt and the moral
culpability of maths or the irrational of anything other than
the positivism of the divine love of Christ but who knows anyway
and it's just like Being or Geist or in the empty set or the knight
of faith or really it's just about the layering of recursive concerns
which are built out from a single state of affairs and the record
of those circumventions and all those radio waves or the various
orbits of a second-order cybernetics and it's actually maybe just
a case of really existing epicycles or the baroque unevenness of
experience and that it's this kind of unevenness that plays at a
certain smoothness or organisation and our understanding of
things starts to be something in and of itself by which I mean it's
that the idea of zero allows for a certain kind of a priori centring
of things and it's that kind of specific pointing that makes things
possible and the symmetry of it which is opposed to the wavering
base of everything that's been lost to history or not and still held
on and still now in the question of debt or in the enacted of our

END PART ONE

13

every day and it's that the poem is still um part of the process

and uh the wind or um slop oatmeal and uhhh debt or it's the
uh implication of the uh empty square or that uh some things
change and that our lives or uh our views and the um uh
propriety of uh knowing and it's like words and days or um
works and these are all things I've said before in other ways
and uh repetition is change and repetitions are uh parts of
the uh process and like uh repetition for stillness which is the
uh reflexivity of it as another uh epicycle extending out from
the um uh experience or uh phenomena or uh but the main
conceit of all this is that the uh implication of the poem is
not limited to the uh literary or the poem itself or even the
interpretation of the uh poem or uh reading and there's a
wider mass of things to uh and it's the things that remain

BEGINNING PART TWO

14

outside of the poem or maybe more accurately it's the outside

of the writing of the poem which is the conditionality of
writing just like as in the reading of the poem or the readers
all of which is just to ignore the naturalness of speech or
writing or maybe not the naturalness of writing or speech
in the way that that the poem is constituted in the field of its
effects and not in the question of language and its like the
way that Pound used to use ideograms and Greek and whatever
else in the multi-vocality of the poem and this is why I was so
interested when Becky was saying that there's something about
the multilingual poem that escapes the academic legitimisation
of the poem as there's no naturalness to be worked against and
it's that there's always some distance to the process of writing

and the movement of the world around it or the continual
decoherence of things around the occurrence of writing or
not but really this isn't about writing it's about something
else like valences or chemical bonds but really what I'm getting
at here is that maybe there's no strangeness across languages
or systems of code and that it's about the interoperability of
things and that there's not even any strangeness to the idea
except the distance of it or both in the lasting and change or

15

the distance of the poem is what goes on between things

and even then the field of linguistic interaction is broader
than the multi-vocality of it which is nevertheless still an
interesting question in the way that the legitimisation of any
particular mode of
discourse is itself just another part of the field of effects as the
compression that exists in the distance between coding and
decoding as the assumption of compatible materials
and the self-reflection of never being able to decide what's
divergent and what's not and these conversations are only
additive and never differential and there's something to think
about in the entropy of the system even though I'm not sure
exactly how to think about what the bounds of the system
might be if we want to be able to judge the complexity of it

16

which is like looking back at that photo of a man from the 1800s

and trying to understand why he's standing there or what
conditions led him to be having his photo taken
or what he was thinking about or anything all of which is about
the diverse networks of concern and force which in the particular
embodiment of that particular person or the intelligibility of

a particular set of genetic materials which I'm looking at in the
photo all of which depends on the particular 'thereness' of
the experience of the present of the photo and all those conditions
which become assembled in the post-hoc analysis and the feeling
of the past or the feeling of a distance from the past comes in
our own dislocation from those networks of effects and our being
outside of those conditions and relations except in a tenuous
way which is like looking through a keyhole not in an informational
way just having insight through the narrow channel of the photo
but in the lack of a processional connection to that man

17
and it's like the idea of a univocal Being in that when you

think about language there's always this idea of expression
or I mean the expression of the linguistic idea is the media
of the idea and I always wonder about entropy and how
informational density is really about the valuation of sameness
and the 'that there' of rationality is the proposition of ratio-
(which is to repeat thing said more formally by others) nality

18
which as like the poem pointing away and toward the ration-

ality of the hand pointing toward itself which is about the
conjunction and nearness of the event and it's always just a
matter of scale and the memory of the idea that scale is just
the distention or condensation of the same or the vector of
sameness toward itself and the realisation of directionality
where the economic is understood as the remainder against
debt and that any account of debt is against itself in the
selfsame existence standing out along and apart from our
occurrence and even as 'every pair of contraries is somewhere
coinstantiated; and every object coinstantiates at least one

pair of contraries' which is in the impossibility of differentiation
and absence apart from the rigours of the phenomenological

19

and is there a problem in regard to the way that the founding

concepts of 'debt' and 'distance' are about lacking in the
selfsame retrograde formulation of occurrence and can be
opposed to the the solidity of a *ratio*nalised cybernetic of
encryption and the certainty of an additive or the mechanistic
of the manufacture of a causal chain which does not rely on
the back-formation of things which is about the idea of a
univocity and this is pure speculation but there will be
a moment where there is a forgetting of the possibility of an
anticipatory being in favour of the certainty that exists without
the lack of debt and this is the idea of monism par excellence

20

and was there ever even a person called Heraclitus or what

do we really know about this kind of change and it's the subject
or object of change which is the difficulty for any kind of
singular monism in that what does not change is the will to
change and the multiple of change and words and doing
which in the unity of the solitary [solidity] is the differentiation
of identity which in opposition to a monism is never previous
to the condition of opposites or distinctions which are 'reached'
or maybe monism is just a pathological rendering of
technocratic desire along the vector of the simplification
of control or dimensionality where the progress of knowledge
is presented in contrast to a concern for the variety of
forms that are themselves translucent in the present theoretical

21

but I set my glass of water down on the table and a portion

of the kinetic energy reaches my ears along the filled-in
space of the air and the conservation of energy continues
in my thinking about the energy of the glass against the table
as it came from the interaction of gravity and the force of my
arm and how the non-specific dissipation of energy across
and along the dampening of an infinite number of vectors
part of which I expend or put out in writing and which
writing works against which is the singular thinking of the
event as a kind of monism part of which exists particularly
in the perception of it being the wholeness of the system of
observation and I guess it's that we only have access to a
particular form of existence such as Being and never not-
Being or a particular facet of Being such as that portion of
the excitation of the air that reaches back to me from the
movement of my arm and the glass and the material of our
perceptions is always predicated upon the systematic story
of occurrence as we can know it and the tautology is in how
things are always-already different and are always-already

22

pieced together which is to say not from difference but

distance which in the repetition of the thing is the lasting
detail of time as a denial of monism and maybe it's just
that we have to allow some little bit of contradiction as
the possibility of distance is precluded by the radical willing
of a singular material which is like the prohibition raised
by Zeno or I mean it's that if we could see everything all
at once there wouldn't be any sense of distance but it's the
limitation of our view that is the introduction of difference
and I mean it's the same limitation of perspective that

reduces everything to another kind of monism or the stacking
of material against itself or like knowing there is a solidness
to the air around you or that the duration of the earth is a
slow liquid and the melting down of landscapes but what is
change but the material or the thing of monism or not the
bow but the bending as in the dimensionality of things being
multiple and we have to go around things which are not
identified by any accidental or essence of valuation but by
occurrence and the transverse happening in the move of

23

fashion and this I guess is a good time to try to recap anything

that has already been said which is to coalesce things around
the question of distance and how the judgement or supposition
of distance is the limit to any monism as to where distance is
said to count which for us as people is always a pretty straight
forward kind of thing being in the continuation of the species
through the propagation of the individual and we can understand
some of this in the thrown-ness of being which is always specific
to that particular occurrence of the thing and the tension comes
in the reaching out or back toward some other of occurrence
which is not present as in the figure of debt or our understanding
of debt all of which can be re-stated in the difference of the
immediacy of material cause and the lag of a coded expression
which even in the mechanistic function of its interpretation
nevertheless relies on the flows of difference which in a monism

24

is about change and I mean the truth of change is that falseness

does not change or to put it another way it's that object
permanence is undergirded by the differentiating recognition
of permanence as it lasts from one moment to the next and

it's the specificity and unevenness of change that allows for the
manifold of permanence or the vacillation from same to the
same and it's that the unevenness of change allows for the
entanglement of a series of observations in the subjective and
what I want to get at here is the idea of a monism and the total
system including difference and change and permanence and
uh how it's the irregular puncture of the Dionysian against

25

the singular and is anything ever actually simple or isn't it just

that the implication of simplicity is that there's no possibility of
order and that possibility is never a simple thing just like how this
is still just part of the process and I don't want to name anything
or make anything too singular here but it's that the whole idea
of process is about complexity and change is never a processional
thing as it's always as amongst the particulate or the singular
occurrence with distance being philosophical truth or *phys* and
it's the fact that I have don't have any option in this except in
the apparition of some centring idea of a singular subjective truth
which is maybe something to do with the grounding of doubt in
the self or maybe it's the apparition that there's something approp-
riate to a singular consideration or the Apollonian of thought
which is always just used as a kind of ontological veridiction
as in the popular reading of Ockham particularly in contrast to

ACKNOWLEDGEMENTS

For Ken, Eddie, Derek, Anselm, Lou, Issac, Jim, Fred, Nick, Arlo, Andrés, Berni, Dan, Cooper, Eirik, Josh, Michael, Joel, Peter, Julia, Thiago, Don, Chris, Emily, Miles, Stacy, Joe, John, Cori, Steve, Paul, Africa, Jordan, Leire, Rowan, Ed, Maureen, Ed, Luna, Adrian, Martín, Holly, Fred, John, Sam, Josh, Joe, Jessica, Christopher, David, Peter, Rainer, Danny, Charles, Ron, Kevin, Stephen, Richard, Douglas, Deanna, Gillian, Maggie, Jane, Curtis, Anna, Bill, Kristi, Kristen, Anna, Prageeta, David, Reginald, Mark, Anselm, Jonathan, Tom, Emily, Charles, Ron, John, Thomas, John, Bobby, Joseph, Jacob, Joshua, John, Robyn, erica, Sam, and Becky.

Additional lyric provided by Baldwin, Berrigan, Braithwaite, Forché, Hill, Sappho, Winters, Howe, Philips, Shakespeare, Alcock, Johnson, Nietzsche, Kapp, Wilde, Olson, Panh, Donne, Mikolowski, Hopkins, Saroyan, Hamilton, Farago, O'Hara, Berryman, Ginsberg, Herodotus, Pound, Heidegger, Artaud, Johns, Warhol, Hesiod, TensorFlow and NLTK developers, Muñoz, Brownstein, Toscano, Coyne, Map, and others. 'They are filthy, they become filthier still.'

LAY OUT YOUR UNREST

www.ingramcontent.com/pod-product-compliance
Lightning Source LLC
Chambersburg PA
CBHW020908100426
42737CB00045B/1215